# The Cricket in Times Square
## Lit Link

### Grades 4-6

**Written by Nat Reed**
**Illustrated by S&S Learning Materials**

**About the author:**
Nat Reed has been a member of the teaching profession for over 30 years. He is presently a full-time instructor at Trent University in the Teacher Education Program.

**ISBN: 978-1-55495-032-4**
**Copyright 2009**
All Rights Reserved * Printed in Canada

Published in the U.S.A by:
On The Mark Press
3909 Witmer Road PMB 175
Niagara Falls, New York
14305
www.onthemarkpress.com

Published in Canada by:
S&S Learning Materials
15 Dairy Avenue
Napanee, Ontario
K7R 1M4
www.sslearning.com

# At A Glance

| Learning Expectations | Ch 1 | Ch 2 | Ch 3 | Ch 4 | Ch 5 | Ch 6 | Ch 7 | Ch 8 | Ch 9 | Ch 10 | Ch 11 | Ch 12 | Ch 13 | Ch 14 | Ch 15 |
|---|---|---|---|---|---|---|---|---|---|---|---|---|---|---|---|
| **Reading Comprehension** | | | | | | | | | | | | | | | |
| • Identify and describe story elements | • | • | • | • | • | • | • | • | • | • | • | • | • | • | • |
| • Summarize events/details | • | • | • | • | • | • | • | • | • | • | • | • | • | • | • |
| **Reasoning & Critical Thinking Skills** | | | | | | | | | | | | | | | |
| • Character traits, comparisons | • | • | | | • | | | • | | | • | | • | | |
| • Use context clues | • | • | | • | | • | • | | | | • | | • | • | • |
| • Make inferences (why events occurred, characters' thoughts and feelings ) | • | • | • | • | • | • | • | | • | • | • | • | • | • | • |
| • Conduct an interview | | | | | | | | | | • | | | | | |
| • Understand abstract concepts – conscience, revenge, fear, perseverance, self-respect, exaggeration, conflict, etc. | • | | | | | | | • | • | | • | | • | • | • |
| • Develop opinions and personal interpretations | • | | | • | • | • | | • | • | • | • | • | • | • | • |
| • Write a letter/newspaper editorial | | | | | | • | | | | | | | | | |
| • Identify *alliteration* | • | | | | | | | | | | | | | | |
| • Identify/create a *simile* | | • | | | | | | | | | | | | | |
| • Identify a *cliffhanger* | • | | | | | | • | | | | | | | | |
| • Identify an *analogy* | | | | | | | | | | | | • | | | |
| • Identify an *idiom* | | | | | | | | | | | | • | | | |
| • Identify *conflict* | | | | | | | | | | • | | | | | |
| • Identify the *climax* of a story | | | | | | | | | | | | | | | • |
| • Design a plan for a cricket house | | | | | • | | | | | | | | | | |
| • Create a book cover | | | | | | | | | | | | | | • | |
| • Complete a Synopsis | | | | | | | • | | | | | | | | |
| • Complete a Story Map | | | | | | | | | | | | | | | • |
| • Create a storyboard | | | | | | | | | | | | • | | | |
| • Create a KWL Chart | | | | | | | | | • | | | | | | |
| • Create a 5 W's Chart | | | | | | | | | | | | | | • | |
| • Practice research skills | • | • | | • | | | | | | | • | | • | • | |
| **Vocabulary Development, Grammar, & Word Usage** | | | | | | | | | | | | | | | |
| • Identify synonyms, antonyms, and homonyms | | • | | • | • | | | • | • | • | | • | • | • | • |
| • Predict an outcome | | • | | | | | • | | | | • | | | | |
| • Identify syllables | | | • | | | | | | | | | | | | |
| • Identify compound words | | | | | | | | | | | | | • | | |
| • Identify parts of speech | | • | | | | | | | • | • | | | | | |
| • Dictionary and thesaurus skills | • | • | • | • | | • | • | • | • | • | • | • | • | • | • |
| • Use words correctly in sentences | • | • | • | • | • | • | • | • | • | • | • | • | • | • | • |
| • Place words in alphabetical order | | | | | • | | | | | | | | | | |
| • Identify singular/plural | | | | • | | | | | | | | | | | |
| • Identify root words | | | | | | | | | • | | | | | | |
| • Using capitals, correct punctuation | | | | | | • | | | | | | | | | |

# THE CRICKET IN TIMES SQUARE

**by George Selden**

## Table of Contents

# THE CRICKET IN TIMES SQUARE

by George Selden

## Overall Expectations

**The students will:**

- develop their skills in reading, writing, listening, and oral communication.

- use good literature as a vehicle for developing skills required by curriculum expectations: reasoning and critical thinking, knowledge of language structure, vocabulary building, and use of conventions.

- become meaningfully engaged in the drama of literature through a variety of types of questions and activities.

- identify and describe elements of stories (i.e. plot, main idea, characters, setting).

- learn and review many skills in order to develop good reading habits.

- provide clear answers to questions and well-constructed explanations.

- organize and classify information to clarify thinking.

- learn about the dynamics of relationships, empathizing and looking out for others who are going through difficult times, learning unselfishness, and the ability to exercise initiative in difficult circumstances.

- relate events and feelings found in the novel to their own lives and experiences.

- appreciate the importance of friendship, loyalty, and sacrifice in personal relationships.

- learn how that standing up for what one feels is right, is the honorable thing to do.

- appreciate that the growth of one's character often comes through the trials of living.

- learn the importance of dealing with adversity and developing perseverance in the face of difficult experiences.

- state their own interpretation of a written work, using evidence from the novel and from their own knowledge and experience.

# THE CRICKET IN TIMES SQUARE

by George Selden

## Before you read the chapter:

### Chapter 2

The last chapter ends as a real **cliffhanger**. What do you suspect made the sound that Tucker hears? Predict what you think might happen in this chapter.

_____

_____

_____

## Vocabulary:

Using words from this chapter, complete the following crossword puzzle.

| mouse | quality | peculiar | self | cautious | cricket | ants | meadow |
|-------|---------|----------|------|----------|---------|------|--------|
| Papa | subway | Mario | Times | argument | assault | expert | wedged |
| throw | took | keg | thicket | news | Tucker | rot | |
| soothe | chirp | stout | rated | refuse | proud | Square | |

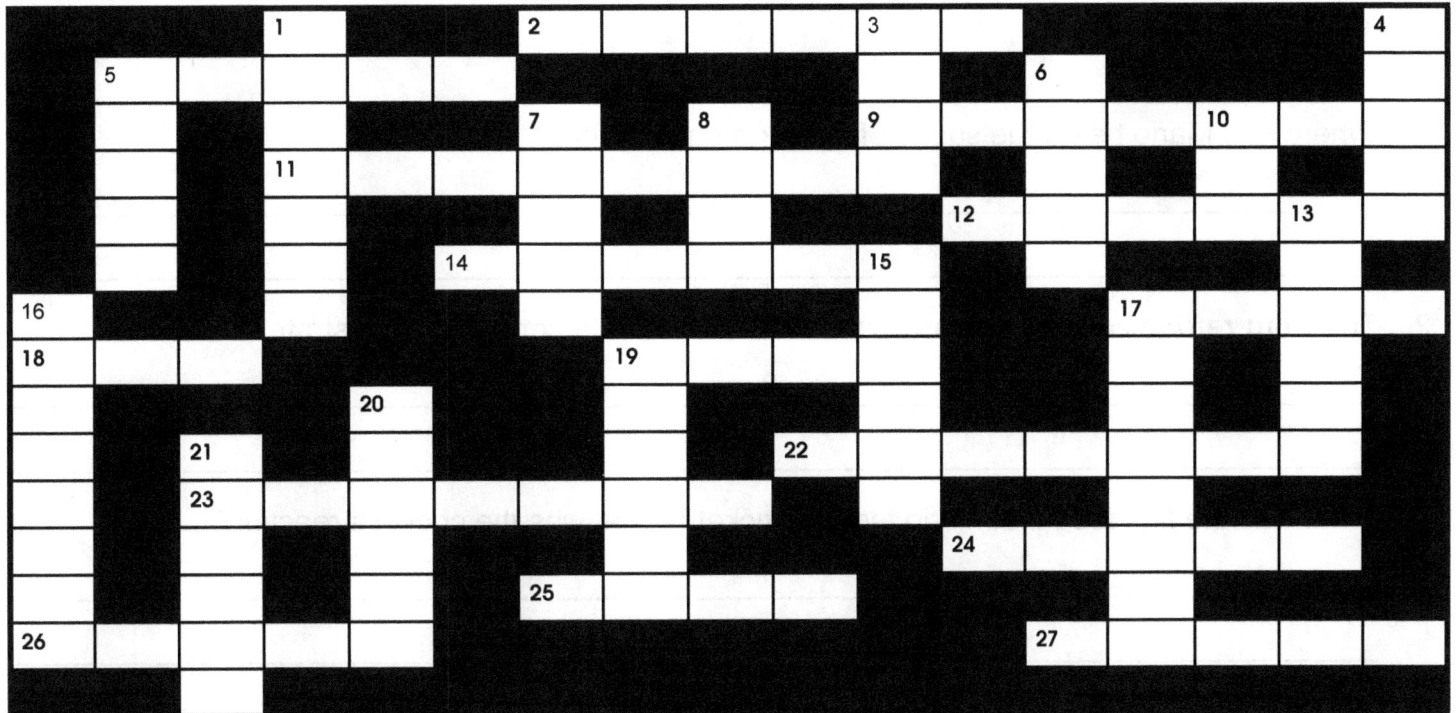

# THE CRICKET IN TIMES SQUARE

by George Selden

| DOWN | ACROSS |
|---|---|
| 1. a chirping insect | 2. a way of city travel |
| 3. busy little insects | 5. the youngest Bellini |
| 4. graded | 9. a dense growth of shrubs |
| 5. Tucker was one of these | 11. careful |
| 6. _____ Square | 12. to pack or fix tightly |
| 7. not thin | 14. the name of a mouse |
| 8. past tense of *take* | 17. Mario's father |
| 10. a small barrel | 18. to undergo decay |
| 13. someone with special skills | 19. a person's nature or character |
| 15. garbage | 22. sudden violent attack |
| 16. a disagreement | 23. grade of excellence |
| 17. odd or unusual | 24. sound of a cricket |
| 19. ease or calm | 25. _____ stand |
| 20. grassland | 26. toss |
| 21. a rectangle having all four sides of equal length | 27. having self-respect |

## Questions???:

1. Where had Mario heard the sound of a cricket once before?

_____

_____

2. The word **refuse** can be used as a verb or a noun. Use a sentence to illustrate each.

_____

_____

3. What was the first food that Mario fed the cricket? What was the cricket's reaction?

_____

_____

# THE CRICKET IN TIMES SQUARE

## by George Selden

4. Put the following sentence in your own words: *There seemed always to be something smiling inside Papa.*

   _____

   _____

5. What did Mama fear might happen if Mario took the cricket home?

   _____

   _____

6. At one point in the story, the author says about Mario, *Just for once, he had been really happy.* Why do you think Mario spent so much time being unhappy?

   _____

   _____

## Language Activities:

A **literary device** the author enjoys using is a **simile** (a comparison using *like* or *as*). An example of this is in the second paragraph when the author writes, "It was like a quick stroke across the strings of a violin, or like a harp that had been plucked suddenly." Here the author is discussing the particular sound made by a cricket. What two things does he compare this sound to?

_____

Come up with three similes of your own that have a definite *Cricket-like* flavor.

_____

_____

_____

_____

# THE CRICKET IN TIMES SQUARE

by George Selden

## Before you read the chapter:

### Chapter 3

What kind of animal do you think makes the best pet? Defend your answer.

_____

_____

_____

_____

Journeying to an unfamiliar place can be a very exciting and scary experience – especially if the traveler is alone. Using your own experiences or your imagination, describe two or three feelings that one might experience when traveling to a completely different place.

_____

_____

_____

## Vocabulary:

In each of the following sets of words, underline the one word that does not belong. Then write a sentence explaining why it does not fit.

1. admire       adore       worship       detest

   _____

2. wistful       resentful       dreamy       longing

   _____

3. selfish       logical       reasonable       rational

   _____

# The CRICKET in TIMES SQUARE

**by George Selden**

4. sympathetic      compassionate      sensitive      aloof

_____

5. cramped      crowded      roomy      confining

_____

6. ecstatic      forlorn      sad      depressed

_____

7. lurch      flounder      careen      stride

_____

8. interrupt      cautious      disrupt      disturb

_____

**Questions???:**

## Cloze Call

Complete the following exercise filling in the correct words from the **Word Box**.

| | | | | |
|---|---|---|---|---|
| liverwurst | musical | Bellini | Mouse | train |
| basket | cat | nervous | days | Tucker |
| dirt | cricket | sandwiches | Connecticut | asleep |

As soon as the _____ family left the newsstand, Tucker _____ ran over to

speak with Chester the _____. Chester had a high, _____ voice. It turned

out that Chester was from _____. He ended up in New York when he was trapped inside

a picnic _____. Chester fell _____ and was trapped when someone placed

a bag of _____ and roast beef _____ on top of him. Chester then traveled

by car, _____, and subway before arriving at the subway station. There Chester lay in a

pile of _____ for two or three _____. At last, Chester became so

# THE CRICKET IN TIMES SQUARE

**by George Selden**

_____ he began to chirp. Chester mentioned that he loved the smell of liverwurst, which

_____ also loved. The chapter came to an exciting conclusion when Chester spotted a

_____ creeping up on them and dove for cover.

## Language Activities:

Choose <u>ten</u> words from this chapter with two or more **syllables**. Indicate the syllables by drawing a line between each syllable. **Example**: **tur/key**.

_____   _____

_____   _____

_____   _____

_____   _____

# THE CRICKET IN TIMES SQUARE

by George Selden

## Before you read the chapter:

## Chapter 4

In Chapter Four, we meet Harry Cat. Mice (like Tucker), of course, are normally prey to cats, yet in this chapter, we find an exception to this rule. If you had a pet cat and introduced another pet into your home which normally would be eaten by the cat (i.e., a mouse or budgie), what steps would you take to make sure the second pet was kept safe?

_____

_____

_____

_____

## Vocabulary:

Draw a straight line to connect the vocabulary word to its definition. Remember to use a straight edge (like a ruler).

1. curious
2. frantic
3. looming
4. acquaintance
5. rapid
6. leery
7. venture
8. refined
9. gradual
10. amid

a. appearing
b. swift
c. dare
d. elegant
e. inquisitive
f. slowly
g. among
h. desperate
i. cautious
j. friend

# THE CRICKET IN TIMES SQUARE

## by George Selden

### Questions???:

1. What was shocking to Chester regarding the relationship between Tucker and Harry?

_____

_____

2. How did Tucker explain his relationship with Harry?

_____

_____

3. Describe how Chester made his special sound.

_____

_____

4. According to Tucker, why was the newsstand going broke?

_____

_____

5. What did Tucker mean by the expression, "long-hairs?"

_____

_____

6. What was Chester's impression of Times Square?

_____

_____

7. At the end of this chapter, what thought was a comfort to Chester?

_____

_____

# THE CRICKET IN TIMES SQUARE

by George Selden

## Language Activities:

Write the plural of the following nouns from this chapter. Careful – you may wish to consult a dictionary for some of these words.

| SINGULAR NOUN | PLURAL NOUN |
|---|---|
| enemy | _____ |
| cat | _____ |
| cricket | _____ |
| city | _____ |
| germ | _____ |
| candy | _____ |
| woodchuck | _____ |
| sky | _____ |
| person | _____ |
| mouse | _____ |

## Extension Activities:

The chirp of a cricket is an appealing sound to many people. It is said that crickets got their name from the French word "Criquer," which means *little creaker*. Another interesting fact about the cricket is that female crickets are deaf! Using resources from your school library or the Internet, investigate the cricket and record three additional facts about this fascinating insect. Illustrate one as well.

_____

_____

_____

_____

_____

# THE CRICKET IN TIMES SQUARE

by George Selden

## Chapter 5

In this chapter, we meet Mickey, who operates a lunch counter in the subway station. What other businesses might be successful in a busy subway station other than a newsstand and lunch counter? Try to think of at least three possibilities.

_____

_____

**Investigate:** In this chapter, it is suggested by one of the characters that **Orpheus** was the greatest musician who ever lived. Using resources in your school library or on the Internet, investigate who Orpheus was, and record three interesting facts about him.

_____

_____

### Vocabulary:

Choose a word from the list that means the same (synonym) or nearly the same as the underlined word.

| | | | | |
|---|---|---|---|---|
| clustered | topple | timid | premonition | expression |
| foretell | ability | peer | delighted | delightful |

1. It is not polite to **look** at someone in that condition. _____
2. I thought for a minute he would **fall** from his ladder. _____
3. It was just a **hunch** that he would arrive on time. _____
4. My sister was **pleased** with her gift. _____
5. She appeared to be a **charming** princess. _____
6. A mouse is usually a very **shy** creature. _____
7. The whole family was **gathered** about the radio. _____
8. His nephew was a person of great **talent**. _____
9. The **look** on the comedian's face made everyone howl. _____
10. I can **predict** that the Angels will win the World Series. _____

# THE CRICKET IN TIMES SQUARE

by George Selden

## Questions???:

1. Describe the strategy that Mario uses in determining what food might appeal to a cricket.

   _____

   _____

2. From what we read of Mickey the Counterman, list one thing we learn of his personality and offer proof to support your answer.

   _____

   _____

3. List the ingredients found in Mickey's cricket strawberry soda.

   _____

   _____

4. Why was Mr. Smedley the Bellinis' best customer?

   _____

   _____

5. What did Mr. Smedley and Mr. Bellini have in common?

   _____

   _____

6. With whom did Mr. Smedley compare Chester. Why?

   _____

   _____

7. As the chapter comes to an end, what did Mario decide he needed to purchase for Chester?

   _____

   _____

# THE CRICKET IN TIMES SQUARE

### by George Selden

## Language Activities:

Place the list of words from this chapter in alphabetical order:

| | | | | |
|---|---|---|---|---|
| cricket | curly | Connecticut | counterman | customer |
| Chester | cash | candy | cup | church |

1. _____
2. _____
3. _____
4. _____
5. _____

6. _____
7. _____
8. _____
9. _____
10. _____

## Extension Activities:

In this chapter, Mario decides to buy a cricket house for Chester. Your task is to design a suitable house for a cricket in the box provided. You may wish to investigate cricket houses to get some ideas of their design, size, etc. Your finished project should contain a drawing and information as to size, color, features, etc.

_____
_____
_____
_____
_____
_____
_____
_____
_____

# THE CRICKET IN TIMES SQUARE

### by George Selden

## Before you read the chapter:

## Chapter 6

In Chapter Six, Mario visits a storeowner, Sai Fong, in Chinatown. Many cities such as New York, feature ethnic areas, where the people of a particular culture live. What would be interesting about visiting such a community as Chinatown in New York City?

_____

_____

_____

## Vocabulary:

Solve the following word search puzzle using the words from the **Word Box**. Remember – the words can be horizontal, vertical or diagonal. They may be forward or even backward!

**Word Box: (15)**

| curious | topple | novelties | pivot | lotus |
|---------|--------|-----------|-------|-------|
| abrupt | remarkable | embroider | ivory | precious |
| lurch | delighted | craned | pagoda | wafer |

| | | | | | | | | | | | | | | |
|---|---|---|---|---|---|---|---|---|---|---|---|---|---|---|
| Q | A | B | R | U | P | T | N | A | D | O | G | A | P | D |
| C | L | W | E | R | T | Y | O | U | I | O | P | A | E | E |
| A | U | S | D | F | G | H | V | J | K | L | A | L | S | M |
| S | R | R | D | W | A | F | E | R | D | F | I | G | H | B |
| Q | C | W | I | E | R | T | L | Y | U | G | I | O | P | R |
| I | H | A | S | O | D | F | T | G | H | H | J | P | K | O |
| L | V | Z | X | C | U | V | I | T | B | N | I | M | Q | I |
| O | W | O | E | R | T | S | E | Y | U | V | I | O | E | D |
| T | A | S | R | D | F | D | S | H | O | J | K | L | L | E |
| U | Z | X | C | Y | V | B | N | T | M | Q | W | E | P | R |
| S | E | D | E | N | A | R | C | E | R | T | Y | U | P | I |
| P | R | E | C | I | O | U | S | W | E | R | T | Y | O | U |
| A | S | E | L | B | A | K | R | A | M | E | R | S | T | R |

# THE CRICKET IN TIMES SQUARE

by George Selden

## Questions???:

1. Why hadn't Chester been able to enjoy the sights during his first subway ride in New York City?

_____

_____

2. What was Sai Fong's impression of Chester?

_____

_____

3. Describe the inside of Sai Fong's shop.

_____

_____

4. In Sai Fong's story, why did the wicked men want to kill Hsi Shuai?

_____

_____

5. Why did the high gods change Hsi Shuai into a cricket?

_____

_____

6. Why do you think Sai Fong sold the cricket cage so cheaply to Mario?

_____

_____

# THE CRICKET IN TIMES SQUARE

**by George Selden**

## Language Activities:

Rewrite the following sentences putting in the **correct capitalization** and **punctuation**.

chester rode all the way to new york city in a picnic basket

_____

_____

the chinese man's name was sai fong

_____

_____

why don't you write a letter to president obama

_____

_____

## Extension Activities:

Chester certainly has had some fantastic adventures during his accidental trip to Times Square. Imagine you are Chester and write a brief letter home to a friend describing your adventures thus far.

Dear _____

_____

_____

_____

_____

_____

Sincerely, Chester

# THE CRICKET IN TIMES SQUARE

by George Selden

## Before you read the chapter:

### Chapter 7

This chapter has a rather intriguing title. Predict what you think the chapter will be about judging from this title.

_____

_____

_____

_____

_____

## Vocabulary:

Use each of the following words in a **sentence**. Make sure that the meaning of the word is clear in your sentence.

**browse:** _____

_____

**admire:** _____

_____

**pagoda:** _____

_____

**volunteer:** _____

_____

# THE CRICKET IN TIMES SQUARE

### by George Selden

register: _____

_____

content: _____

_____

hesitate: _____

_____

luxury: _____

_____

## Questions???:

1. How was Harry able to satisfy his love of Chinese food?

   _____

   _____

2. How was Chester released from his cage?

   _____

   _____

3. a) What was one thing that Tucker didn't like about sleeping in the cricket cage?

   _____

   _____

# THE CRICKET IN TIMES SQUARE

**by George Selden**

b) How was this problem solved?

_____

_____

c) What did he use for a pillow?

_____

_____

4. Why do you think sleeping in the cricket cage was so appealing to Tucker?

_____

_____

## Language Activities:

1. The author ends this chapter on a note of suspense. This is a literary device known as a **cliffhanger**. Predict what you think might happen when the Bellinis arrive at the newsstand in the morning.

_____

_____

_____

_____

2. Imagine that while sleeping in the cricket cage, Tucker has a most interesting dream. What might Tucker dream about? Using your imagination, write a **synopsis** of Tucker's dream.

_____

_____

_____

_____

# THE CRICKET IN TIMES SQUARE

by George Selden

## Chapter 8

Describe a time in your life when you made a mistake and were forced to pay the consequences for your actions. Do you think the consequences were fair for all concerned?

_____

_____

_____

_____

## Vocabulary:

Choose a word from the list to complete each sentence.

| | | | | |
|---|---|---|---|---|
| honorable | stalling | stern | disgusting | unsavory |
| fetch | furious | forlorn | evidence | concentrate |

1. "Gertrude, will you please _____ my slippers for me?" he asked.

2. The quarterback was _____ when the opposing player grabbed the face guard of his helmet.

3. The little boy had the most _____ look on his face when his parents left him at summer camp for the week.

4. Someone who is honest and upright is said to be an _____ person.

5. It is impossible for my niece to _____ for more than a few minutes at a time.

6. The amount of garbage that has accumulated in your bedroom is really quite _____.

7. The principal gave everyone in the cafeteria a very _____ look.

# THE CRICKET IN TIMES SQUARE

**by George Selden**

8. What _____ do they have that he is the guilty party?

9. As a member of that notorious gang, he is believed to be a most _____ character.

10. "Quit _____ and give me the answer to my question," he shouted.

## Questions???:

1. a) At the beginning of this chapter, describe Chester's dream.

_____

_____

   b) What was he actually doing in his sleep?

_____

_____

2. a) Why was Mrs. Bellini's arrival at the newsstand so unexpected for Chester and Tucker?

_____

_____

   b) What was the result?

_____

_____

3. a) What consequence did Mario face as a result of Chester's actions?

_____

_____

   b) Do you think this is a fair decision? Explain your answer.

_____

_____

# THE CRICKET IN TIMES SQUARE

**by George Selden**

4. What solution did Harry, Tucker, and Chester come up with for replacing the missing money?

_____

_____

## Extension Activities:

Choose any two characters you've already met in this novel. Compare four things about these two characters. Consider such things as physical appearance, personality, age, talents, attitude, etc. Give a complete description for each point of comparison.

| | Character 1<br>Name: _____ | Character 2<br>Name: _____ |
|---|---|---|
| 1. | | |
| 2. | | |
| 3. | | |
| 4. | | |

# THE CRICKET IN TIMES SQUARE

by George Selden

## Before you read the chapter:

## Chapter 9

Meeting people from another culture can be a very interesting experience. Mario has such an opportunity in this chapter. How might it be good for a person to meet people from other cultures on a regular basis?

_____

_____

_____

## Vocabulary:

**Synonyms** are words with similar meanings. Using the context of the sentences below, circle the best synonym for the underlined words in each sentence.

1. Isabelle was wearing a <u>lavender</u> dress.
   a) red             b) purple           c) blue           d) green

2. The old Chinese man gave Mario a <u>solemn</u> bow.
   a) half            b) slow             c) honest         d) dignified

3. "That was an excellent <u>deduction</u>, John," the teacher said.
   a) conclusion      b) painting         c) story          d) solo

4. The event was a little more <u>formal</u> than Jennifer thought it would be.
   a) expensive       b) dressy           c) comical        d) dated

5. After the visit, Chester felt very <u>contented</u>.
   a) disoriented     b) exhausted        c) satisfied      d) hyper

6. The policeman was very <u>dismayed</u> to learn of the robbery.
   a) concerned       b) excited          c) curious        d) overjoyed

7. Chester <u>peered</u> into the cage.
   a) stumbled        b) walked           c) hurried        d) looked

# THE CRICKET IN TIMES SQUARE

**by George Selden**

## Questions???:

1. At the beginning of the chapter, what problem does Mario realize he might have with his new pet?

_____

_____

2. With whom did Mario go to consult about this problem?

_____

_____

3. Why do you think the old Chinese man was delighted when he heard Chester chirping?

_____

_____

4. Why do you think they put a Chinese robe on Mario before they ate supper?

_____

_____

5. What suggestion did Sai Fong make to help Mario with the chopsticks?

_____

_____

6. What did the book suggest that crickets enjoyed eating? Where did Mario discover he could get this food for Chester?

_____

_____

# THE CRICKET IN TIMES SQUARE

by George Selden

## Language Activities:

1. Copy out any three sentences from this chapter and underline the **verbs**.

   _____

   _____

   _____

   _____

2. Beside each of the following words from this chapter, write its **root word**.

   a) rapped _____    e) said _____

   b) singing _____    f) dabbing _____

   c) putting _____    g) bowed _____

   d) excitement _____    h) going _____

3. The word "bow" can be used as a **noun** or a **verb**, depending on the sentence. Use your imagination and write sentences to illustrate how this word can be used as both a **noun** and a **verb**.

   **BOW**

   noun: _____

   _____

   verb: _____

   _____

# THE CRICKET IN TIMES SQUARE
## by George Selden

## KWL Chart

So far, this novel has presented a number of interesting topics for the reader to consider: **crickets, mice, cats, New York City, Connecticut, Italian opera**, and **subways** are a few examples. Choose one of these topics (or another one from the novel) and then in the first column below write down *what you already know* about the topic. Then in the second column write down *what you would like to find out* about the topic. Finally, investigate the topic in your school library or the Internet and see if you can uncover what you wanted to know, and other interesting facts about the topic of your choice.

Topic: _____

| What I Know | What I Want to Know | What I Learned |
|---|---|---|
|  |  |  |

# THE CRICKET IN TIMES SQUARE

by George Selden

## Chapter 10

Parties can be a lot of fun. In this chapter, Chester attends a party thrown in his honor. What do you think are three essential ingredients of a successful party?

_____

_____

_____

_____

**Vocabulary:**

**Antonyms** are words with opposite meanings.

**A**. Draw a line from each word in column A to its antonym in column B.

| Column A | Column B |
|----------|----------|
| curious | calm |
| perfect | disinterested |
| furious | casual |
| encourage | disrespect |
| amateur | flawed |
| formal | professional |
| admiration | dishearten |

**B**. Now use the words in Column A to fill in the blanks in the sentences.

1. The butler was most _____ when greeting the guests.

2. I have nothing but _____ for someone with his goodness and generosity.

3. Only _____ players are allowed to enroll in the tournament.

# THE CRICKET IN TIMES SQUARE

### by George Selden

4.  He did everything he could to _____ his daughter to improve her grades.

5.  The little chipmunk was very _____ to see what was inside the box.

6.  When the bucket of water was dumped on the principal's head, he was so _____

    he couldn't even speak.

7.  That figure skater's routine was as _____ as you will ever see.

## Questions???:

Indicate whether the following statements are **True** or **False**.

1.  The animals decided to have a party to celebrate Chester's six month
    anniversary of being in New York.                                        T or F

2.  Tucker provided everyone with iced soft drinks.                          T or F

3.  Harry Cat had just returned from a Rolling Stones concert.               T or F

4.  Harry's singing was enjoyed by Tucker and Chester.                       T or F

5.  Chester's feelings were badly hurt when the other animals did not enjoy his
    playing.                                                                 T or F

6.  Tucker started the fire by knocking a box of matches onto the floor.     T or F

7.  Harry blocked the escape hole when he pushed a bunch of magazines off a
    shelf and onto the floor.                                                T or F

8.  Chester managed to get help by setting off the alarm clock.              T or F

# THE CRICKET IN TIMES SQUARE

**by George Selden**

## Language Activities:

Find three examples of the following parts of speech from this chapter.

| Nouns | Verbs | Adjectives |
|-------|-------|------------|
| _____ | _____ | _____ |
| _____ | _____ | _____ |
| _____ | _____ | _____ |

## Extension Activities:

1. **Interview** at least three other students for their views of this novel thus far. (Try to get both positive and negative comments.) Write a brief **report** putting these views together.

   _____

   _____

   _____

   _____

   _____

   _____

2. **Investigation**: the author mentions Harry attending a concert at **Washington Square**. Research **Washington Square** in your school library or on the Internet and try to find out a couple of interesting details about this famous landmark.

   _____

   _____

   _____

# THE CRICKET IN TIMES SQUARE

**by George Selden**

## Extension Activities:

3. We have already read about a number of important conflicts in this novel. Conflict is an important element in a novel. There are generally three types of conflict: person against person; person against self; and person against nature. Find three examples of conflict in The Cricket in Times Square and tell which type of conflict each is. (You don't have to get an example from each category.)

A. _____

_____

_____

_____

_____

B. _____

_____

_____

_____

_____

C. _____

_____

_____

_____

_____

# THE CRICKET IN TIMES SQUARE

by George Selden

## Before you read the chapter:

## Chapter 11

Sometimes in life, it is tempting to take the easy way out, even when we know it is the wrong thing to do. In this chapter, Chester does the honorable thing by staying and facing the consequences for his role in starting the fire in the newsstand. Tell of time when you or a friend did the honorable thing by facing the consequences for something you did, even though you knew it would be difficult.

_____

_____

_____

_____

## Vocabulary:

**Analogies** are equations in which the first pair of words has the same relationship as the second pair of words.  For example, **stop** is to **go** as **fast** is to **slow**. In this example, both pairs of words are opposites. Choose the best word from the word box to complete each of the analogies below.

| avid | increase | feeling | protect | encourage |
|------|----------|---------|---------|-----------|
| pace | honor | devastation | joyous | fade |

1. **Defend** is to _____ as **sharp** is to **keen**.

2. **Destruction** is to _____ as **smart** is to **intelligent**.

3. **Subside** is to _____ as **best** is to **worst**.

4. **Disheartened** is to _____ as **long** is to **short**.

5. **Eager** is to _____ as **gate** is to **entrance**.

6. **Disgrace** is to _____ as **love** is to **hate**.

# THE CRICKET IN TIMES SQUARE

### by George Selden

7. **Slow** is to **sluggish** as **dwindle** is to _____.

8. **Frightening** is to **terrifying** as **tempo** is to _____.

9. **Loud** is to **boisterous** as **emotion** is to _____.

10. **Stop** is to **go** as **downhearted** is to _____.

## Questions???:

1. Why did Chester go back into the newsstand after the fire?

   _____

   _____

2. Why do you think the Bellini family took a taxi only in emergencies?

   _____

   _____

3. What did it mean when Mama folded her arms across her chest?

   _____

   _____

4. When Chester played the song, "Come Back to Sorento," of what did it remind Mama?

   _____

   _____

5. Describe the circumstances that changed Mama's attitude about Chester staying.

   _____

   _____

   _____

# THE CRICKET IN TIMES SQUARE

by George Selden

## Language Activities:

1. An **idiom** is a literary device that says one thing, but means another (i.e., *you hit the nail on the head*). An example from this section is *the words were drowned in Mama's flood of reproaches*. Think of another example of an **idiom** and record it below. (Your example does not have to be from the novel.)

   _____

   _____

   _____

2. This chapter ends on a very suspenseful note, stating that the coming week would be *the most remarkable week in Chester Cricket's – or any cricket's life*. Predict how you think events will unfold in the coming days to make it such a remarkable week for Chester.

   _____

   _____

   _____

   _____

# THE CRICKET IN TIMES SQUARE

by George Selden

## Before you read the chapter:

### Chapter 12

Different types of music are mentioned in this novel: opera, musical comedies, hymns, etc. What type of music do you enjoy the most? Why is this type of music your favorite?

_____

_____

_____

_____

## Vocabulary:

Choose a word from the list to complete each definition:

| | | | | |
|---|---|---|---|---|
| hesitate | suspicious | comedy | prefer | rodent |
| sensitive | triumphant | privilege | implore | sublime |

1. A _____ belongs to the gnawing or nibbling mammal family.

2. To **like better** is to _____.

3. To be **distrustful** or **doubtful** is to be _____.

4. If something is said to be _____, it is very impressive.

5. To pause or falter is to _____.

6. The winner of an event or competition is _____.

7. A _____ person is commonly tactful and diplomatic.

8. To _____ someone is to beg them.

9. To be favored is to have _____.

10. The opposite of drama is _____.

# THE CRICKET IN TIMES SQUARE

by George Selden

## Questions???:

1. What three understandings did Tucker outline at the beginning of the chapter?

   _____

   _____

   _____

2. What did Chester's formal musical education consist of?

   _____

   _____

3. Why did Chester choose a hymn to begin his concert to the Bellinis?

   _____

   _____

4. Describe Mr. Smedley's reaction to Chester's playing.

   _____

   _____

5. **Investigate**: What does the term "absolute pitch" mean?

   _____

   _____

6. Why do you think the author refers to Chester as a "person?"

   _____

   _____

# THE CRICKET IN TIMES SQUARE

by George Selden

## Antonyms, Synonyms or Homonyms

Beside each pair of words, write **A** (antonym) or **S** (synonym) or **H** (homonym).

1. be - bee _____
2. friend - pal _____
3. do - dew _____
4. broke - mend _____
5. first - last _____

6. moist - dry _____
7. hymn - him _____
8. illustrious - magnificent _____
9. new - knew _____
10. not - knot _____

Choose a pair of antonyms, a pair of synonyms and a pair of homonyms and use each word in a sentence to show its meaning.

**Antonyms**: _____

Sentences: _____

_____

_____

**Synonyms**: _____

Sentences: _____

_____

_____

**Homonyms**: _____

Sentences: _____

_____

_____

# The Cricket in Times Square
by George Selden

## Storyboard

A storyboard is a series of pictures that tell the main events of a story. A storyboard can tell the story of only one scene – or the entire novel.

Complete the storyboard below illustrating your favorite scene from **The Cricket in Times Square** thus far. You may wish to practice your drawings on a separate piece of paper.

| 1. | 2. |
|---|---|
| 3. | 4. |
| 5. | 6. |

# THE CRICKET IN TIMES SQUARE

by George Selden

If you had read Mr. Smedley's letter to the editor about Chester, do you think you would have been curious enough to go down to the Times Square subway station to see this unusual insect? Why or why not?

_____

_____

_____

_____

_____

## Vocabulary:

Replace the words, that are underlined in the sentences below, with a word from the word list in the box. Remember to consider the context of the word in the sentences, as some words may have several meanings.

| | | | | |
|---|---|---|---|---|
| intermission | souvenir | delighted | throngs | celebrity |
| recital | anxious | selection | delicacy | tempt |

1. Everyone in the restaurant grew quiet when the **famous person** entered. _____

2. Alonzo was very **happy** to be invited to the party. _____

3. Sophie made an unusual **choice**. _____

4. **Crowds** of people entered the square to hear the astronaut's speech. _____

5. The opera singer's **performance** was breathtaking. _____

# THE CRICKET IN TIMES SQUARE

### by George Selden

6. To a cricket, mulberry leaves are a real **treat**. _____

7. They went out for a breath of fresh air during the **break**. _____

8. She purchased a postcard as a **memento** of her visit to the Alamo. _____

9. Do you think that the low price will **entice** buyers? _____

10. Public speaking causes most people to be **apprehensive**. _____

## Questions???:

1. What is an *entomologist*?

   _____

   _____

2. **Investigate**: a composition by **Mozart**, "A Little Night Music," is mentioned in this chapter. In your school library or on the Internet, research three interesting facts about this gifted man.

   _____

   _____

   _____

3. How were the Bellinis able to take advantage of the crowds attending Chester's concerts?

   _____

   _____

4. After Mr. Smedley's letter, what further publicity did Chester receive?

   _____

   _____

# THE CRICKET IN TIMES SQUARE

by George Selden

5  The author says, "Mama Bellini, by the way, turned out to be the best friend a cricket ever had." How was this true?

_____

_____

6  Why wasn't Chester happy anymore?

_____

_____

7  **Reading between the lines**. Read the last paragraph in this chapter again. What do you think Chester has made up his mind to do?

_____

_____

## Language Activities:

Try to reassemble the word parts listed below into ten compound words found in these chapters.

| sub | body | sides | way | break | one | news | side | box | every |
|-----|------|-------|-----|-------|-----|------|------|-----|-------|
| stand | out | him | some | cricket | be | fast | self | napper | match |

1. _____     6. _____

2. _____     7. _____

3. _____     8. _____

4. _____     9. _____

5. _____     10. _____

# THE CRICKET IN TIMES SQUARE

by George Selden

## The Five W's Chart

Choose a major event from **The Cricket in Times Square**, then complete the following chart with the appropriate details.

**What happened?**

_____

_____

_____

**Who was there?**

_____

_____

_____

**Why did it happen?**

_____

_____

_____

**When did it happen?**

_____

_____

_____

**Where did it happen?**

_____

_____

_____

# THE CRICKET IN TIMES SQUARE

**by George Selden**

## Before you read the chapter:

## Chapter 14

An ancient Chinese proverb says, "A Wise man makes his own decisions, an ignorant man follows public opinion." How might this proverb apply to Chester's situation at this time in his life?

_____

_____

_____

## Vocabulary:

Choose a word from the list to complete each sentence.

| | | | | |
|---|---|---|---|---|
| scuttled | fidgeted | content | flustered | fascinated |
| melody | pleasure | gesture | dreadfully | summit |

1. There was little doubt that the sight of the bank robber _____ the teller.

2. The little girl _____ restlessly while her mother filled the car with gas.

3. The orchestra conductor gave a dramatic _____ at the conclusion of the concert.

4. The two mountain climbers reached the _____ of the highest peak in Asia.

5. I will be _____ sorry to see Chester go.

6. It was a real _____ to meet her mother.

7. The trio of animals _____ across the busy lobby.

8. The audience was _____ with the magician's *slights of hand*.

9. Mario was perfectly _____ to listen to Chester's playing for hours on end.

10. The song's _____ was very beautiful and complicated.

# THE CRICKET IN TIMES SQUARE

**by George Selden**

## Questions???:

1. Why do you think the author gave this chapter the title, "Orpheus?"

_____

_____

2. What was there about September that made Chester feel sad?

_____

_____

3. What evidence did Chester have that the animals from his home in Connecticut liked to listen to his playing?

_____

_____

4. Why do you think Chester and Tucker both felt that Friday was an excellent day to retire on?

_____

_____

5. Why did Chester choose "Lucia di Lammermoor" as his final piece?

_____

_____

6. What effect did Chester's final piece have on the crowd and a good part of the city?

_____

_____

# THE CRICKET IN TIMES SQUARE

by George Selden

## Extension Activities:

Create a **book cover** for <u>**The Cricket in Times Square**</u>. Be sure to include the title, author, and a picture that will make other students want to read the novel.

# THE CRICKET IN TIMES SQUARE

by George Selden

## Before you read the chapter:

## Chapter 15

Saying goodbye to friends can be a very difficult experience. Describe a time in your life when you had to say goodbye to someone close to you. Be sure to mention how it made you feel.

_____

_____

_____

_____

## Vocabulary:

Draw a straight line to connect the vocabulary word to its definition. Remember to use a straight edge (like a ruler).

| | | | |
|---|---|---|---|
| 1. | smidgen | a. | stifle |
| 2. | expression | b. | searching |
| 3. | familiar | c. | utterance |
| 4. | muffle | d. | appointment |
| 5. | maze | e. | eased |
| 6. | rummage | f. | a little bit |
| 7. | relieved | g. | cupboard |
| 8. | abrupt | h. | all of a sudden |
| 9. | engagement | i. | labyrinth |
| 10. | pantry | j. | acquainted |

# THE CRICKET IN TIMES SQUARE

by George Selden

### Questions???:

1. What two games did Mario and Chester play in this chapter?

   _____    _____

2. Why do you think Chester gave a private recital to Mario?

   _____

   _____

3. Why did Chester take the bell from the cash register?

   _____

   _____

4. Why did Chester ride on Harry's back?

   _____

   _____

5. How did Mario know that Chester was gone and wouldn't be back?

   _____

   _____

6. The climax of a story occurs when the main problem of the story is solved. When does the climax of the novel occur?

   _____

   _____

7. Describe your feelings about this novel. What was one thing you really enjoyed, and one thing you think that the author might have improved upon?

   _____

   _____

   _____

   _____

# THE CRICKET IN TIMES SQUARE

by George Selden

## Story Map

Complete the following Story Map from the reading of **The Cricket in Times Square**.

| Setting | |
|---|---|
| Approximate Time: | Place: |

| Characters | |
|---|---|
| Major: | Minor: |

| Problem/Challenge |
|---|
| |

| Plot/Events (At least six items) |
|---|
| |

| Resolution (Climax) |
|---|
| |

## Chapter 1 (Page 10)

**Vocabulary:**

| | | | | |
|---|---|---|---|---|
| 1. scrounge | 2. abandoned | 3. subsided | 4. vanished | 5. gust |
| 6. Niche | 7. grilles | 8. shuttle | 9. displayed | 10. pity |

**Questions:**
1. Sleeping and watching the world go by.
2. He had to go to bed early on weekdays.
3. Times Square.
4. It got stuck once with all their money in it.
5. He bought a paper and gave Mario a 25 cent tip. *Answers will vary.*
6. *Answers will vary.* (i.e., the sound of rain, babies crying)
7. A cliffhanger is a literary device in which the chapter ends suddenly leaving the reader in suspense.
   *Answers will vary.*

**Language Activities:** *Answers will vary.*

## Chapter 2 (Page 13)

**Vocabulary:**

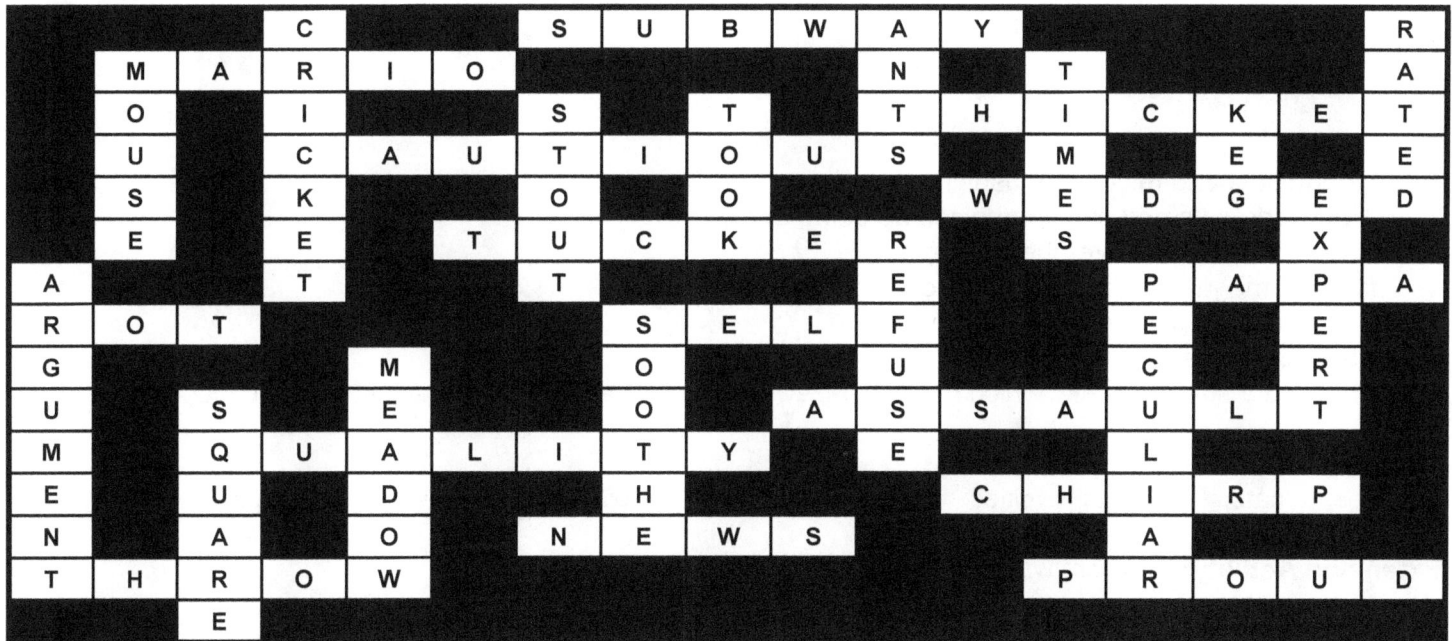

**Questions:**
1. In a meadow on Long Island the summer before.
2. *Answers will vary.* i.e, <u>Noun</u>: The garbage can was filled with **refuse**. <u>Verb</u>: He didn't dare **refuse** to obey the principal.
3. A piece of chocolate bar. He enjoyed it.
4. *Answers will vary.* i.e., Papa always seemed to be happy.
5. The cricket might attract other insects.
6. *Answers will vary.* Perhaps he was lonely.

**Language Activities:**
a harp and violin

**Chapter 3 (Page 16)**

**Before you read the chapter:** *Answers will vary.*

**Vocabulary:**
| | | | | |
|---|---|---|---|---|
| 1. detest | 2. resentful | 3. selfish | 4. aloof | 5. roomy |
| 6. ecstatic | 7. stride | 8. cautious | | |

**Questions:**
As soon as the <u>Bellini</u> family left the newsstand, Tucker Mouse ran over to speak with Chester the <u>cricket</u>. Chester had a high, <u>musical</u> voice. It turned out that Chester was from <u>Connecticut</u>. He ended up in New York when he was trapped inside a picnic <u>basket</u>. Chester fell <u>asleep</u> and was trapped when someone placed a bag of <u>liverwurst</u> and roast beef <u>sandwiches</u> on top of him. Chester then traveled by car, <u>train</u>, and subway before arriving at the subway station. There Chester lay in a pile of <u>dirt</u> for two or three <u>days</u>. At last, Chester became so <u>nervous</u> he began to chirp. Chester mentioned that he loved the smell of liverwurst, which <u>Tucker</u> also loved. The chapter came to an exciting conclusion when Chester spotted a <u>cat</u> creeping up on them and dove for cover.

**Language Activities:** *Answers will vary.*

**Chapter 4 (Page 19)**

**Before you read the chapter:** *Answers will vary.*

**Vocabulary:**
1. e   2. h   3. a   4. j   5. b   6. i   7. c   8. d   9. f   10. g

**Questions:**
1. Although cats and mice were usually natural enemies, Tucker and Harry were best friends.
2. In New York, cats and mice had given up being enemies.
3. He drew his top wing over the bottom one.
4. They sold magazines that appealed only to a few "long-hairs."
5. An extra-refined person.
6. It was too terrible and beautiful for a cricket from the country.
7. He noticed a star in the sky which he recognized as one he had looked at back in Connecticut.

**Language Activities:**
enemies;   cats;   crickets;   cities;   germs;   candies;   woodchucks;   skies;   people;   mice

**Extension Activity:** *Answers will vary.*

**Chapter 5 (Page 22)**

**Vocabulary:**
| | | | | |
|---|---|---|---|---|
| 1. peer | 2. topple | 3. premonition | 4. delighted | 5. delightful |
| 6. timid | 7. clustered | 8. ability | 9. expression | 10. foretell |

**Questions:**
1. He tried him out on everything.
2. *Answers will vary.* i.e., He was kind, giving both Mario and Chester free sodas.
3. A drop of strawberry syrup, a drop of cream, a squirt of soda water, and a dip of ice cream.
4. He bought Musical America.
5. They loved Italian opera.

6. Orpheus, because he was the greatest musician who ever lived.
7. A house (or cage).

## Language Activities:
1. candy
2. cash
3. Chester
4. Church
5. Connecticut
6. counterman
7. cricket
8. cup
9. curly
10. customer

## Chapter 6 (Page 25)

**Before you read the chapter:** *Answers will vary.*

## Vocabulary:

| Q | A | B | R | U | P | T | N | A | D | O | G | A | P | D |
|---|---|---|---|---|---|---|---|---|---|---|---|---|---|---|
| C | L | W | E | R | T | Y | O | U | I | O | P | A | E | E |
| A | U | S | D | F | G | H | V | J | K | L | A | L | S | M |
| S | R | R | D | W | A | F | E | R | D | F | I | G | H | B |
| Q | C | W | I | E | R | T | L | Y | U | G | I | O | P | R |
| I | H | A | S | O | D | F | T | G | H | H | J | P | K | O |
| L | V | Z | X | C | U | V | I | T | B | N | I | M | Q | I |
| O | W | O | E | R | T | S | E | Y | U | V | I | O | E | D |
| T | A | S | R | D | F | D | S | H | O | J | K | L | L | E |
| U | Z | X | C | Y | V | B | N | T | M | Q | W | E | P | R |
| S | E | D | E | N | A | R | C | E | R | T | Y | U | P | I |
| P | R | E | C | I | O | U | S | W | E | R | T | Y | O | U |
| A | S | E | L | B | A | K | R | A | M | E | R | S | T | R |

## Questions:
1. He was buried under sandwiches in a picnic basket.
2. He was very impressed with Chester.
3. It was very cluttered.
4. Hsi Shuai spoke the truth and told everyone how wicked the men were.
5. To save his life.
6. *Answers will vary.* (i.e., He supported Mario's love of the cricket.)

## Language Activities:
Chester rode all the way to New York City in a picnic basket.
The Chinese man's name was Sai Fong.
Why don't you write a letter to President Obama?

## Chapter 7 (Page 28)

**Vocabulary:** *Answers will vary.*

## Questions:
1. By browsing through the garbage cans in Chinatown.
2. Harry used one of the nails of his right forepaw to lift the latch to the gate of the cage.
3. a) The floor was a little hard to sleep on.
   b) They got a dollar bill from the cash register for him to sleep on.
   c) One of Mama Bellini's earrings.
4. *Answers will vary.* (i.e., He felt rich and important – like he was sleeping in a mansion.)

**Language Activities:** *Answers will vary.*

## Chapter 8 (Page 31)

**Before you read the chapters:** *Answers will vary.*

**Vocabulary:**
1. fetch      2. furious      3. forlorn      4. honorable      5. concentrate
6. disgusting      7. stern      8. evidence      9. unsavory      10. stalling

**Questions:**
1. a) He was back in Connecticut eating a willow leaf.
   b) He was eating a two-dollar bill.
2. a) The animals were in the middle of a conversation.
   b) She threw a magazine at Tucker and hit him on the leg.
3. a) Chester would be confined to his cage until Mario repaid the two dollars.
   b) *Answers will vary.*
   c) One of Mama Bellini`s earrings.
4. They replaced the two-dollars from Tucker's savings.

**Extension Activities:** *Answers will vary.*

## Chapter 9 (Page 34)

**Before you read the chapter:** *Answers will vary.*

**Vocabulary:**
1. b) purple      2. d) dignified      3. a) conclusion      4. b) dressy      5. c) satisfied
6. a) concerned      7. d) looked

**Questions:**
1. A problem with Chester's diet.
2. Sai Fong.
3. *Answers will vary.*
4. *Answers will vary.* (Perhaps to make him feel at home.)
5. Make believe the chopsticks were two long fingers.
6. Mulberry leaves. Sai Fong had a mulberry tree just outside his window.

**Language Activities:**
2. a) rap    b) sing    c) put    d) excite    e) say    f) dab    g) bow    h) go

**Extensions Activities:** *Answers will vary.*

## Chapter 10 (Page 38)

**Before you read the chapter:** *Answers will vary.*
**Vocabulary:**
A. curious - disinterested; perfect – flawed; furious - calm; encourage – dishearten;
   amateur – professional; formal - casual; admiration - disrespect.
B. 1. formal      2. admiration      3. amateur      4. encourage      5. curious
   6. furious      7. perfect

**Questions:** 1. False   2. True   3. False   4. False   5. False   6. True   7. True   8. True

**Language Activities:** *Answers will vary.*

## Chapter 11 (Page 42)

**Before you read the chapter:** *Answers will vary.*

**Vocabulary:**

| | | | | |
|---|---|---|---|---|
| 1. protect | 2. devastation | 3. increase | 4. encourage | 5. Avid |
| 6. honor | 7. fade | 8. pace | 9. feeling | 10. joyous |

**Questions:**
1. If the Bellinis found him gone, they would think he set the fire and ran.
2. They were poor and taking a taxi was costly.
3. There was no point in arguing with her – her mind was made up.
4. Of being back in Naples and being courted by Papa.
5. *Answers will vary.* Her attitude against keeping Chester was softened by his playing.

**Language Activities:** *Answers will vary.*

## Chapter 12 (Page 45)

**Before you read the chapter:** *Answers will vary.*

**Vocabulary:**

| | | | | |
|---|---|---|---|---|
| 1. rodent | 2. prefer | 3. suspicious | 4. sublime | 5. hesitate |
| 6. triumphant | 7. sensitive | 8. implore | 9. privilege | 10. comedy |

**Questions:**
1. Chester is a very talented person; talent is something rare, beautiful and precious; there might be a little money in it.
2. One evening of learning different numbers from the radio.
3. It was Sunday.
4. *Answers will vary.* He was shocked.
5. Also known as **perfect pitch**, it is the ability of a person to identify or recreate a musical note without the benefit of a known reference.
6. *Answers will vary.*

**Language Activities:**
1. H　2. S　3. H　4. S　5. A　6. A　7. H　8. S　9. H　10. H

## Chapter 13 (Page 49)

**Before you read the chapter:** *Answers will vary.*

**Vocabulary:**

| | | | | |
|---|---|---|---|---|
| 1. celebrity | 2. delighted | 3. selection | 4. throngs | 5. recital |
| 6. delicacy | 7. intermission | 8. souvenir | 9. tempt | 10. anxious |

**Questions:**
1. An insect expert.
2. *Answers will vary.*
3. They were able to sell more papers.
4. Other newspapers ran articles; Musical America sent an editor to do a story and his story was featured on

radio and television news.

5. She fixed him delicious meals.
6. He was lonely for his home in the country; he didn't like the crowds always looking at him.
7. *Answers will vary* (i.e., return home to Connecticut).

**Language Activities:**

| | | | | |
|---|---|---|---|---|
| newsstand | breakfast | himself | somebody | everyone |
| subway | besides | outside | matchbox | cricketnapper |

## Chapter 14 (Page 53)

**Vocabulary:**

| | | | | |
|---|---|---|---|---|
| 1. flustered | 2. fidgeted | 3. gesture | 4. summit | 5. dreadfully |
| 6. pleasure | 7. scuttled | 8. fascinated | 9. content | 10. melody |

**Questions:**

1. *Answers will vary.* (i.e., He may be insinuating that cricket is now the world's finest musician).
2. *Answers will vary.* (i.e., He knew the trees would be changing in Connecticut, and he missed his home there).
3. *Answers will vary.* (i.e., The bullfrog told him. When a fox was chasing a rabbit, they both stopped to listen to him.)
4. *Answers will vary.* (i.e., It was the end of the work week.)
5. It was Papa's favorite.
6. They were silent while they listened.

**Extension Activities:** *Answers may vary.*

## Chapter 15 (Page 56)

**Vocabulary:**
1. f    2. c    3. j    4. a    5. i    6. b    7. e    8. h    9. d    10. g

**Questions:**

1. Hide-and-seek; jumping where Mario placed his hand.
2. *Answers will vary.* (i.e., to thank him and say good-bye).
3. It was his, and he wanted something to remember the Bellinis by.
4. It was faster and safer.
5. He had taken the bell.
6. *Answers will vary.* (i.e., when Chester gives his final public concert).
7. *Answers will vary.*

**Extension Activity:**
**Story Map**
<u>Setting</u>: Times Square, New York City.  Fairly recently
<u>Characters</u>: Major – Chester, Tucker, Harry, Mario
<u>Minor</u>: Mama and Papa Bellini, Sai Fong, Mr. Smedley
<u>Problem</u>: Chester the Cricket ends up in Times Square.
<u>Plot</u>: (*Answers will vary.*) Chester is discovered. He makes friends with Tucker and Harry. They discover he is a gifted musician. They almost burn the newsstand down. Chester is discovered. He gives his last public performance. Chester leaves for Connecticut.
<u>Resolution</u>: Chester makes up his mind about returning home and gives his last concert.